Mary
MOTHER OF JESUS

The Story of Mary
accurately retold from the Bible
(from Matthew, Mark, Luke and John), by
CARINE MACKENZIE

Design and Illustrations
Mackay Design Associates Ltd

Published in Great Britain by
CHRISTIAN FOCUS PUBLICATIONS LTD
Geanies House, Fearn, Tain, Ross-shire IV20 1TW, Scotland
http://www.christianfocus.com
© 1980 Christian Focus Publications Ltd ISBN 0 906731 06 2

New edition 1989
Reprinted 1992
Reprinted 1998

Mary was a young Jewish woman who lived long ago in the country of Galilee. She was soon to be married to a man called Joseph.

One day Mary had an important visitor. The angel Gabriel came and gave her a message from God. "You are going to have a baby boy", he said, "and you will call him JESUS".

"How can that happen to me?" Mary asked, "I am not married yet".

The angel then told Mary that her baby would be very special. He was to be made by the powerful work of the Holy Spirit inside her body and he would be called THE SON OF GOD as well as JESUS.

The angel also told her, "Your cousin Elizabeth is going to have a baby boy too. Everybody thinks she will never have a baby because she is so old, but her baby will be born soon".

Mary believed that God would do these amazing things.

Mary then went to visit Elizabeth, who lived with her husband Zacharias.

As soon as she arrived at Elizabeth's home, Elizabeth said, "Blessed are you among women and blessed is your child". Elizabeth knew about Mary's baby already because God had told her and she believed.

Mary also showed that she believed for she began to praise the Lord in a beautiful song which begins:
"My soul doth magnify the Lord".

She believed that God was now sending His Son Christ Jesus to be the Saviour, as He had promised long ago.

Mary knew that she needed a
Saviour to save her from her sins.
We all need to have our sins
forgiven. The only one who can
save us is Jesus the Saviour.

Mary and Joseph got married and
lived in the town of Nazareth.

Joseph worked as a carpenter and Mary looked after the house. I am sure that she was also getting clothes ready for her baby.

One day Joseph said, "I have some news for you, Mary. We have to go to Bethlehem right away to do some very important business".

It took them a few days to travel the long journey from Nazareth to Bethlehem.

Many other travellers had come to Bethlehem and the inn was full. Joseph and Mary could not find a proper place to stay so they had to use the part of the inn where the animals slept.

It was there that Mary's baby was born. What great joy she must have felt. How tenderly and lovingly she looked after him.

She wrapped him up snugly and put him in a safe and warm place, in the manger, to rest and sleep.

Soon afterwards, Mary and Joseph and their baby were visited by some shepherds.

The shepherds came because an angel visited them as they watched their flocks at night and said, "I bring you good news. A Saviour has been born today in the city of David. He is Christ the Lord".

Mary was amazed at what the shepherds told her, and she often thought about it afterwards.

It was the law of the Jews, that when the first baby boy was born in a family, the mother and father had to go to the temple to make an offering to the Lord. So Mary and Joseph went to the temple at Jerusalem. They took baby Jesus with them.

In the temple they met a good old man called Simeon. He had been told by God that he would not die until he had seen Jesus Christ, the promised Saviour.

When he saw Mary and Joseph with their baby, Simeon knew that at last he was looking at the Saviour.

He took Jesus in his arms and praised the Lord. "Now I am ready to die", he said, "for I have seen the Saviour of sinners". Simeon then blessed Mary and Joseph.

After Mary, Joseph and Jesus went back to Bethlehem they had more visitors. These were wise men, from a country in the East. They had seen a strange star in the sky and believed this meant that the king of the Jews had been born. So they went to Jerusalem to see him, but they could not find him.

King Herod heard about the wise men looking for the new baby. He was very jealous and angry because he heard that Jesus was a king.

The wise men then travelled on to Bethlehem and the star kept moving in front of them. It stopped right over the house where Mary and the young baby were! The wise men worshipped Jesus and gave him beautiful presents.

Soon afterwards King Herod did a terrible thing. He killed many of the babies in Bethlehem. He thought he would be sure to kill baby Jesus this way.

But Jesus was safe for God had told Joseph, "Take Jesus and Mary and go to Egypt and stay there".

After Herod died Joseph took Mary
and Jesus back to Nazareth.

Every year Mary and Joseph went to Jerusalem to attend the Passover Feast. They took Jesus for the first time when he was twelve years old. When they were going home from the feast, Mary and Joseph discovered that Jesus was not with them.

They searched everywhere but
they could not find him. How
worried they were. They went right
back to Jerusalem and searched
there too. At last they found
him. He was in the temple.

Jesus told them that he had
stayed at the temple because he
had to do his Father's work.

Mary did not understand that
Jesus was speaking about his
heavenly Father, God.

Afterwards, as Jesus grew up, she
often thought about what he had
said.

One day, many years later, Mary and Jesus were invited to a wedding in the town of Cana.

During the feast the servants discovered that the wine was finished.

What would they do? Mary came and said to Jesus, "They have no wine left".

She then told the servants to do whatever Jesus said.

"Fill these water pots with water", Jesus told them. "Now take some of it to the man in charge of the feast".

The man tasted it and called to the bridegroom, "This is good wine!"

Mary knew that Jesus had changed the water into wine.

Once, when Jesus was speaking to a crowd of people, a woman shouted to him, "Blessed is the woman who gave birth to you and who fed you as a baby".

Jesus told her that those who hear and keep God's word are really blessed.

So we see that Jesus taught that Mary was no more blessed than others who obey His word.

Some time later Mary got very sad news. She heard that Jesus had been captured by wicked men who were going to kill him. They hated him and so they nailed him to a cross.

Mary could do nothing to help him but she kept as near him as she could while he was suffering on the cross.

Although Jesus was in very great pain, he was sorry for his mother and wanted to help her. He told John, his disciple, to look after Mary as if she were his own mother. Jesus showed his love for his mother even when he was dying. So Mary stayed at John's home, and he looked after her.

Mary was still very sad however,
for Jesus had died on the cross
and was then buried in a grave
called a sepulchre.

Very soon afterwards Mary heard astonishing news. Some of her friends went to the sepulchre and they found it empty. They hurried back to tell the disciples.

Peter and John then ran to the sepulchre. Yes, it was empty! When John went back to his house, I am sure he told Mary all about the empty grave.

But where was Jesus? Jesus was alive! He had risen from the dead three days after his burial and he visited his disciples and dear friends before he went back to heaven.

Mary spent a lot of time with these friends after Jesus went up to heaven. They used to meet together for worship in an upstairs room in Jerusalem. Mary and her other sons were often there.

Mary was a meek and humble woman. She was a tender and loving mother. She was a sinner who put her trust in the Saviour, the Lord Jesus Christ.

We are all sinners too but Jesus is alive today and is able to save us from our sins. We must put our trust in the Saviour, just as Mary did.